Forty sparkling qu[...] aspects of the Sixties. Designed to delight, bemuse and bewilder, SIXTIES TRIVIA is a quiz-book in which the answers are infinitely more interesting than the questions! What's more, the daftest answers are usually the right ones!

Also available:

QUOTABLE TRIVIA
SHOWBIZ TRIVIA

NIGEL REES

SIXTIES TRIVIA

London
UNWIN PAPERBACKS
Boston   **Sydney**

First published by Unwin Paperbacks, 1985

This book is copyright under the Berne Convention.
No reproduction without permission. All rights reserved.

UNWIN® PAPERBACKS
40 Museum Street, London WC1A 1LU, UK

Unwin Paperbacks
Park Lane, Hemel Hempstead, Herts HP2 4TE, UK

George Allen & Unwin Australia Pty Ltd
8 Napier Street, North Sydney, NSW 2060, Australia

Unwin Paperbacks with the
Port Nicholson Press
PO Box 11-838 Wellington, New Zealand

© Nigel Rees Productions Ltd, 1985

ISBN 0 04 793082 9

Set in 10 on 11 point Souvenir by Nene Phototypesetters Ltd
and printed in Great Britain by
The Anchor Press Ltd, Tiptree, Essex

For Thelma – and all who were there

CONTENTS

Preface

QUESTIONS

ANSWERS

PREFACE

The subject of trivia is important. As I hope will be made clear by this book, trivia can be a potent reminder of times past and often more potent than recollections of major events.

I have observed, however, that what passes for 'trivia' in quizzes like these are often *not trivial enough*. So I have made a special effort to seek out those minor – but evocative – gobbits of information that should bring it all flooding back (whatever 'it' may be).

Some of the questions are ball-crackingly difficult. So, to alleviate the pain, may I suggest you insert a finger in the back without further delay?

NIGEL REES

QUESTIONS

ABSOLUTELY TRIVIAL!

1 What complaint did Judy Geeson have when she appeared in *Emergency Ward Ten*?

2 In 1968, 'I'm Backing Britain' T-shirts were discovered to have been manufactured in which country?

3 What is the connection between Jim, Genevieve and Magpie?

4 Tim Rice failed to win the *Ready Steady Go!* 'Look-Alike' competition. Who was he trying to look like?

5 What was the name of the group of which Tim Rice was the lead singer when he was at school? (Clue: it would have been ahead of Abba.)

6 What is the connection between Peter Hawkins and 'Let's Go To San Francisco'?

7 What sort of girl did Joe Brown and Marty Wilde both marry?

8 Give one interesting fact about Joe Brown's origins.

9 Stubby Kaye loved to cry at weddings – but why was it a case of 'Didn't he do well!' when it came to his own?

10 Whose first stage-names were Johnny Silver, Paul Ramon, Carl Harrison and Stu de Stijl, respectively?

ADS

1 He was never alone with a Strand and had his own fan club – but nobody bought the product. Who was he?

2 The Jim Webb song 'Up, Up and Away' was used to promote which airline?

3 Complete the jingle: 'Rael-Brook Toplin, The . . .'

4 The 'Get Away People' used which brand of petrol?

5 Why did tiger-tails adorn the nation's cars?

6 'Happiness is . . .' was a theme of much Sixties advertising. How did it originate?

7 'Award yourself the C.D.M.' But what did the initials stand for?

8 What was 'Cool as a Mountain Stream'?

9 Who said 'Roses grow on you'?

10 By what name was Mary Holland better known? (Clue: she was married to Philip.)

BEATLEMANIA

1 What was the name of the Beatle brother who had a No. 1 hit?

2 Who was the Beatle relative who tried to have a hit with 'That's My Life'?

3 Who was dubbed 'the Fifth Beatle' by Murray the K?

4 Who were married in Gibraltar and then held a week-long 'Bed-In for Peace' at the Amsterdam Hilton?

5 Richard Buckle described the Beatles as 'the greatest composers since ————'?

6 Tony Palmer called the Beatles 'the greatest songwriters since ————'?

7 What was John Lennon's middle name?

8 What did the Queen Mother say when the Beatles told her their next engagement was in Slough?

9 What were the Blue Meanies?

10 What is said *not* to have happened during the Beatles' first US TV appearance?

BEEB

1 *The Troubleshooters* was a BBC drama series about an oil company which was shown from 1965–70. What was the original name of the show?

2 *An Age of Kings* was a brilliant series broadcast in 1960 and based on Shakespeare's history plays from Richard II to Richard III. Who played (a) Henry V and (b) Harry Hotspur?

3 *Till Death Us Do Part* was a comedy series broadcast with great success from 1964–74. What was the name of the equally successful US-TV version?

4 In the early 60s, what was the name of the man who helped spearhead the great Do-It-Yourself boom?

5 What did U.N.C.L.E. mean in *The Man from U.N.C.L.E.*?

6 Who were Hullabaloo and Custard and what happened on the first night?

7 What is the connection between the title of the signature tune of *Steptoe and Son* and the producer of *That Was The Week That Was*?

8 What was the name of the horse in *Steptoe and Son*?

9 Who lost a bit of himself when knighted and insisted on 'homosexual' being pronounced with a short 'o'?

10 Why should you not confuse *Dig This!* with *Dig This Rhubarb*?

BESTSELLERS

1 How many times does the word f——— or f———g appear in *Lady Chatterley's Lover* – at least according to the prosecuting counsel?

2 How much did a copy of the unexpurgated Penguin edition of *Lady Chatterley's Lover* cost in 1960?

3 Who were 'Maxwell Kenton'? Their most famous novel end with the words 'Good grief – it's Daddy!'

4 In which of Ian Fleming's James Bond novels – published in 1961 and filmed in 1965 – does Bond score a 'most satisfactory left and right' of Miss Patricia Fearing on the squab seats from her bubble car high up on the Downs near Brighton?

5 *Colonel Sun* was a James Bond 'sequel' written in 1968 by 'Robert Markham' – what well-known writer lay behind that pen-name?

6 Who published *Last Exit to Brooklyn* in Britain?

7 Who wrote *Honest to God*?

8 'She was so deeply inbedded in my consciousness that for the first year of school I seem to have believed that each of my teachers was my mother in disguise' – first words of a novel. What was this a symptom of?

9 What was the title of John Lennon's *second* book?

10 'The temperature hit ninety degrees the day she arrived. New York was steaming . . .' – first words of a novel first published in 1966. It was to sell over 28 million copies during the next eighteen years. What is it called?

BOND WOMEN

1 Who played 'Honeychile Rider' in *Dr No*?

2 Who played 'Tatiana Romanova' in *From Russia with Love*?

3 What was the name of the less than lovely character played by Lotte Lenya in the same film?

4 Who played 'Pussy Galore' in *Goldfinger*?

5 And whatever happened to Shirley Eaton?

6 Who played 'Domino' in *Thunderball*?

7 Who played 'Kissy Suzuki' in *You Only Live Twice*?

8 Who played 'Giovanna Goodthighs' in *Casino Royale*?

9 Who played 'Tracy Draco' in *On Her Majesty's Secret Service* – and was glad that she fell under a bus?

10 Who played the ever-frustrated 'Miss Moneypenny' in all the films?

CATCHPHRASES

1 Which *Laugh-In* catchphrase did Richard Nixon say on the programme broadcast in the US on 16 September 1968?

2 Who might have said of 'The Wednesbury Madison' – 'I'll give it foive'?

3 In which film does James Bond *himself* first ask for a 'martini – shaken not stirred'?

4 'Seriously, though, he's doing a grand job' – who said so?

5 Who said 'I'm in charge'?

6 What was Arte Johnson wearing on his head when he said, 'Verrry interesting . . . '?

7 Which radio programme had you 'either been listening to – or just missed'?

8 'Letters, we get letters, we get stacks and stacks of letters' – who did?

9 'You dirty old man' – who said it of whom?

10 'Bernie the Bolt' – said who?

FAB GEAR

1 Who went to Buckingham Palace in a mini-skirt to collect her OBE in 1965? (Clue: she shaved her pubic hair into a heart-shape.)

2 In what year was the 'Way In' department opened at Harrods?

3 What did John Stephen do with men's trousers?

4 How do you know when you are in Carnaby Street? (Old joke.)

5 Who said: 'Hair is another name for sex'?

6 What did people do with winkle-pickers?

7 Which face ended up in the 1980s running a Cornish hotel noted for its 'utterly acceptable mild eccentricity'?

8 What had Mr Fish to do with kippers?

9 Who founded Biba, the boutique that turned into a superstore and flopped?

10 In 1968, what was 16-year-old Jayne Harries wearing that prevented her entering the Royal Enclosure at Ascot?

FADS

1 In which year was the Ford Cortina Mk 1 introduced and how much did it cost?

2 In which year did the first Kentucky Fried Chicken open in London?

3 1966 saw the opening of Britain's first drive-in lion reserve. Where was it?

4 What was celebrated by the 'Gonk Song' (sung by the Gonks) and by the film *Gonks Go Beat* (in 1965)?

5 What was IT?

6 What happened at 144 Piccadilly?

7 '——— are hippies who have been hit on a head by a policeman' (Jerry Rubin). Who were?

8 Why were 'Mods' so called?

9 Where is Haight-Ashbury?

10 What was lysergic acid diethylamide more usually called?

FILMS

. . . i.e. 'movies' made on this side of the
Atlantic . . .

1 Who directed *It's Trad, Dad* before he got the
knack?

2 Who went from Big Fry to Big Screen?

3 What darling made her first screen appearance in
Billy Liar?

4 Who made her acting debut and exit in *Privilege*?

5 A sign for whose shop appears at the beginning of
The Servant?

6 Which actual London park was the setting for the
'incident' in *Blow-Up*?

7 With whom did Albert Finney play the celebrated
'eating' scene in *Tom Jones*?

8 What sport was featured in *This Sporting Life*?

9 Which 1966 film – set in the nineteenth century –
clearly showed TV aerials over the Royal Crescent
in Bath?

10 What sort of job did Peter O'Toole have before he
landed the part of *Lawrence of Arabia*?

FROSTIE

1 What is David Frost's middle name?
(*Not* 'money'!)

2 Is he the son of an Anglican vicar, a Methodist minister, or a Jewish rabbi?

3 What is his mother's name?

4 What was the title of the first network TV programme he appeared on in-vision?

5 The first edition of the BBC TV programme *That Was The Week That Was* was transmitted on 24 November 1962. The *Radio Times* billing mentioned six supporting cast, little known then, well known now. What were their names?

6 Who was originally to have introduced *TW3*?

7 Who composed Frostie's theme tune? (Clue: its title is 'By George! The David Frost Theme'.)

8 In the 60s, Frostie's name was romantically linked with several women. Which of the following did he actually marry? – Janette Scott, Diahann Carroll, Karen Graham.

9 Who called him 'the Bubonic Plagiarist'?

10 What did Harold Wilson, the Bishop of Woolwich, Len Deighton, and Cecil King – among others – do with Frostie on 8 January 1966?

GROUPS

1 Why are the Bee Gees so called?

2 What did Adolf Hitler play, according to 'The Intro and the Outro'?

3 And what was Roy Rogers on?

4 Who had a hit in the charts for a grand total of fifty-five weeks from November 1961 with the theme tune from a 1959 children's TV series? (Unhelpful clue: in the recording studio that day was a diminutive actress who later told the *News of the World*, 'I am that twentieth-century failure – a happy undersexed celibate.')

5 Complete the line-up of the group headed by Dave Dee that had hits with 'Bend It' and 'Legend of Xanadu'. (NB Names must appear in the correct order.)

6 When the Dave Clark Five had hits like 'Glad All Over' and 'Bits and Pieces' in 1963/4, it was suggested that the Mersey Sound was being replaced by the ——— Sound?

7 The Monkees was the name of a pop group created for an American TV series and designed to emulate the Beatles, 1966/8. Name the four singers and – er – musicians.

8 One of them had previously acted in *Coronation Street*. Which one?

9 Another had appeared as a child actor in the title role of a 50s American TV series called *Circus Boy*. Which one?

10 'A Whiter Shade of Pale' was a No. 1 hit for Procul Harum in May 1967. What does Procul Harum mean?

GRUESOME
TWOSOMES

1 Who said 'Sock it to me' to Burt Reynolds?

2 Who were the 'B & K' of British politics (i.e. not Bulganin and Khruschev)?

3 Who featured in the Divorce of the Century in 1963?

4 What did Cotton and Clore have in common?

5 Peter and Gordon and Paul and Jane. Who was related to whom?

6 Who was David Bailey's first wife?

7 Who was Anouk Finney?

8 Which twins had a pet snake called Nipper?

9 Which twins had a famous father and a brother who was to be called 'the cleverest young man in England'?

10 Which couple played a couple and invited a couple to play 'Get the Guests'?

HACKS

1 Name the three editors of the 'schoolkids' edition of *Oz* – tried at the Old Bailey for obscenity in 1970, although they hadn't edited it?

2 In which year did *The Times* first put news on its front page?

3 To what issue did an editorial in *The Times* headed 'It *Is* A Moral Issue' refer?

4 In which year did the *Sun* rise?

5 Who was the first editor of *Private Eye*?

6 Which four-letter women's magazine started in 1965 was noted for having more male than female readers?

7 What was the name of the seven-letter women's magazine featured in a twice-weekly BBC TV soap opera?

8 Who occasioned the Newspaper Proprietors' Association changing its name to the Newspaper Publishers' Association?

9 'Prince Philip and the Profumo Scandal' was a *Daily Mirror* headline in 1963. What was the story underneath?

10 What sort of journalism did Tom Wolfe, Gay Talese and Nicholas Tomalin – among others – practise?

I LIKE THE BACKING

Name the group that backed the following singers (i.e. Freddie and the *Dreamers*).

1 Billy J. Kramer and the ———?

2 Bob Dylan and the ———?

3 Buddy Holly and the ———?

4 Lulu and the ———?

5 Joe Brown and his ———?

6 Mike Berry with the ———?

7 Gary Puckett and the ——— ———?

8 Kenny Rogers and the ——— ———?

9 B. Bumble and the ———?

10 Ray Davies and the ———?

LENNON AND McCARTNEY

. . . and their compositions:

1 In which song did the Beatles sing 'Yeah yeah yeah'?

2 When Peter Sellers performed 'A Hard Day's Night' who was he impersonating?

3 How did he perform 'Help'?

4 What record does 'Yesterday' hold?

5 Which Lennon and McCartney song was played at playwright Joe Orton's funeral?

6 On which Beatles LP does Paul sing 'Her Majesty's a pretty nice girl but she doesn't have a lot to say'?

7 Which album begins with John Lennon announcing 'Charles Hawtrey and the Deaf Aids'?

8 Who was 'Hey Jude' originally addressed to?

9 Which song names two British Prime Ministers?

10 How many holes are there in Blackburn, Lancashire?

LIVERPOOL

1 Who said (*c.*1964): 'Liverpool is at the present moment the centre of the consciousness of the human universe'?

2 Which Liverpool parliamentary constituency did a Prime Minister represent in the 1960s?

3 Which group featured in the film *Ferry Across the Mersey*?

4 What – opened in 1967 – was known as 'Paddy's Wigwam'?

5 What is/are Strawberry Fields?

6 Where are jam butty mines located?

7 What did Maggie May do – though not very well on stage?

8 Roger McGough, Adrian Henri and Brian Patten were members of The Scaffold. True or false?

9 Which of the following people were *not* born in Liverpool: Kenny Everett, Robert Robinson, Jimmy Tarbuck, Nerys Hughes, Polly James, Cilla Black, Ken Dodd?

10 According to tradition, what are the birds on the Liver Building supposed to do when passed by a woman of untarnished virtue?

M.O.R.

Middle-of-the-road music . . .

1 Who was the singing bus driver? (Clue: his route was the No. 27 from Highgate to Teddington.)

2 Who was the fastest milkman in the west?

3 Who, of the following, has never *sung* on a record: Jimmy Savile, Tony Blackburn, Alan Freeman, Emperor Rosko?

4 Who ate it up and spat it out?

5 Who was Marlene Dietrich's musical director during her 1964 London season? (Clue: she said, 'I can't love him any more than I love him now'.)

6 Who sang 'Bye Bye Blackbird' outside the Houses of Parliament in 1968?

7 'Moon River' was the theme from which film?

8 Who recited 'Deck of Cards'?

9 Rolf Harris accompanied himself on a —— —— in 'Tie me Kangaroo Down Sport'.

10 Which songstress won *Opportunity Knocks* in 1968?

MOVIES

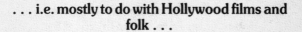

... i.e. mostly to do with Hollywood films and folk ...

1 What was wrong with the 1968 film *Krakatoa, East of Java*?

2 What film, released in 1966, consisted entirely of grunts and gave rise to a memorable poster of a scantily clad Raquel Welch?

3 Which Czech-born actor spent two weeks in September with Brigitte Bardot, went behind the camera for Mae West, and then went back in?

4 Who used to talk to a wooden-headed fellow and then was widely seen enthusing over 'brown paper packages tied up with strings'?

5 In which 60s film did Robert Redford and Jane Fonda co-star?

6 On 31 July 1963 Mandy Rice-Davies attended the London premiere of which famous film?

7 Which was Marilyn Monroe's last *completed* film?

8 Who was Steve McQueen's female lead in *Bullitt*?

9 Which film star is generally considered to be the subject of Carly Simon's song 'You're So Vain'?

10 In which film would you have heard the song 'Windmills of Your Mind'?

NEWS TOENAILS

1 How much money was stolen in the Great Train Robbery? (a) £2½ million (b) £5 million (c) £1¼ million?

2 He was on the loose for twelve days in 1965; there were sixty-five BBC bulletins about him; and 5,000 people came to London to look at him. He attacked a dog called Dusty. When he was caught, the *Sun* brought out a souvenir edition. Who was he?

3 Describe the Beeching Axe in one sentence.

4 What did Hattie do in the Caribbean in 1961?

5 What did Marilyn Monroe do to President Kennedy in the middle of Madison Square Garden in 1962?

6 What event in space was celebrated by Joe Meek with a double first on earth?

7 What 'first' took place between Rhyl and Wallasey in July 1962 – without touching earth?

8 What was the name of the astronaut who did *not* step on the moon in July 1969?

9 Why did the Duke of Wellington appear in a Bond movie?

10 Who ordered a glass of cherry brandy in a pub in 1963?

NICKNAMES

Who was known as . . . ?

1 'The Thinking Man's Crumpet'. (Clue: she brought a touch of blue stocking to colour TV.)

2 'Little Miss Dynamite'?

3 'Fluff' (and why? All right? Right!)

4 'Danny Le Rouge'?

5 'The Galloping Gourmet'?

6 'Diddy David'?

7 'The Shrimp'?

8 'The Houdini of Politics'?

9 'Mad Mitch'?

10 And, why was he called Clarence 'Frogman' Henry?

OLDIES BUT GOLDIES

Memorable songs . . .

1 Where would you have hesitated to leave a cake out in the rain – and where is it?

2 'They've changed our local Palais into a bowling alley' – because?

3 Who sang 'Up Je T'aime'?

4 What happens when the man comes on the radio and is telling me more and more about some useless information supposed to fire my imagination?

5 'Goodness Gracious Me', recorded by Peter Sellers and Sophia Loren in 1960, was based on characters they played in which film?

6 Who sang something stupid together?

7 What did Gerry and the Pacemakers take from the fairground to the terraces?

8 What other hit did The Chiffons' 'He's So Fine' 'inspire'?

9 When did we 'skip the light fandango' and the crowd call out for more?

10 'Hallelujah, I love her so' – who said so?

OTHER CHANNEL

ITV programmes and personalities . . .

1 In which series did the character of John Steed (Patrick MacNee) first appear?

2 Why was 'Emma Peel' so called?

3 Germaine Greer once appeared regularly in a TV show with Kenny Everett. What was it called?

4 Who invented *Coronation Street*?

5 The Thames TV jingle, first heard in 1968, is based on an old London air. Which one?

6 Who were the presenters of *Ready Steady Go!*?

7 The first TV news bulletin in Britain to feature two newscasters was ITN's *News at Ten*, first broadcast on 3 July 1967. Who were they on that occasion?

8 What was the name of the Italianate Welsh village where much of *The Prisoner* was filmed?

9 Who was the host of *Stars and Garters*?

10 Who hosted a late-night show on ITV, took it with him to the BBC, and then had to give it up for cream of tomato?

PERMISSIVE SOCIETY

Sexual barriers came down almost as frequently as knickers in the 1960s – or so they say . . .

1 Who loved Mick Jagger and Mars bars?

2 What was all right after July 1967 – if you were so inclined?

3 What was the connection between Yoko Ono and Corbett Woodall, a BBC TV newsreader?

4 A woman dressed from tip to toe in leather and a man dressed in Edwardian gear hymned the praises of kinky boots. Who were they?

5 In the Beatles' song, who was the original of 'Sexy Sadie'?

6 When Mandy Rice-Davies said, 'Well, he would, wouldn't he?' – who was 'he'?

7 Who first said 'f——' on British TV?

8 Which cinema film is thought to have been the first to reveal pubic hair – in 1966?

9 Whose record simulating orgasm got to No. 1 in October 1969 while being banned by the BBC?

10 Concerning which book did a bishop say in 1960 that a sex relationship was shown in it as 'essentially sacred . . . as in a real sense an act of holy communion'? (Clue: it always fell open at page 34.)

PERSONALITIES

1 Who stuttered his way to success in *Not So Much A Programme, More A Way of Life*?

2 And who was Harvey Orkin?

3 What did General Loan do? (It wasn't very nice.)

4 What did Viv Nicholson say she was going to do in 1961?

5 Who installed a coin-box phone for visitors to his home in 1961?

6 David Hicks, interior designer, married whose daughter?

7 What did Gertrude Shilling start doing?

8 Who was the former rep actress who set more than a hundred light aircraft records?

9 Distinguish between Bo Diddley and Bo Dudley.

10 Who were given a plot of land in Mustique as a wedding present in 1960?

POLITICS

1 When Willie Rushton stood against Sir Alec Douglas-Home in the Kinross by-election in 1963, what party did he represent and how many votes did he get?

2 Which politician was made to sing 'She Wouldn't Say Yes' by *Private Eye*?

3 Who disclaimed his peerage in order to become Prime Minister, but needn't have bothered?

4 Who became Prime Minister and then disclaimed his peerage and by what title was he known when a boy?

5 Who was 'paid more for impersonating Harold Wilson than Harold Wilson'?

6 How do you translate the Russian for shoe-banging – and when was this necessary?

7 Who provided the Gannex, became a peer, and went to prison?

8 Who ran the World Domination League?

9 Anthony Wedgwood-Benn couldn't wait to disclaim his peerage (or his hyphen, for that matter) – what title did he have?

10 For what purpose did Harold Macmillan enter King Edward VIII's Hospital for Officers in October 1963?

POP NAMES

By what names do we know these people better?

1 Mary O'Brien. (Clue: she had a brother called Dion O'Brien who also made a name for himself.)

2 Bernard Jewry. (Clue: he picked up a dead colleague's 'Shane', is called 'Bert' by his wife, and has a very confused mother.)

3 Priscilla White.

4 Richard Starkey.

5 Gerald James. (Clue: he had pullover trouble.)

6 Ernest Evans. (Clue: he contrived to make a name like Fats Domino.)

7 Gerry Dorsey.

8 Thomas Woodward. (Clue: he took his name and his pigtail from a popular film.)

9 Marie Macdonald Lawrie.

10 Herbert Khaury. (Clue 1: he was married on Johnny Carson's *Tonight* show. Clue 2: earlier stagenames had included Dary Dover, Emmett Swink, and Larry Love the Singing Canary.)

POP RADIO

1 Who provided TV on Radio? (Clue: his name was Richard West.)

2 Whose was the first voice on Radio 1 and what was the first record he played and why couldn't he take his eyes off you?

3 Why did David Pilditch sing 'A Special Goodnight to You'?

4 Joe Pasternak's son Mike had a title. What was it?

5 Whose son said 'Groovy Baby'? (Clue: Dave Wish helped him.)

6 What did Ronan O'Rahilly do to President Kennedy's daughter?

7 Carl Henty-Dodd and Anthony Killick both sang 'Julie'. Who were they?

8 Who was Raymondo – and did you know that Max Alcock was half of him?

9 Just before the Light Programme gave way to Radio 1 in 1967, who was the last person to present *Housewives' Choice*?

10 Who used to begin Saturday mornings with a cheery, 'Hello, me old mates'?

POP SINGERS

1 Who was a welder's daughter from Dagenham – so short-sighted that she couldn't see she'd left something behind?

2 Who was the first British pop singer to stand for parliament? And when?

3 This Danish baroness eventually left her baron and, in the 70s, shacked up with a fraud. Who was she?

4 Davie Jones and the King Bees came from Bromley and Beckenham. In 1964 they recorded 'Liza Jane' but he didn't get his act together until 1969. Who was he?

5 Who was the bird to whom Mike Sarne sang 'Come Outside' in May 1962? She ended up minding the store.

6 Why did James Marcus Smith split his pants at the Ritz Cinema, Luton, in February 1965?

7 An actor appearing in the ITV soap opera *Harpers West One* sang 'Johnny Remember Me' in 1961 and rapidly discovered he had a real No. 1 hit on his hands. Who was he?

8 Who was on a TV gig with the Archbishop of York in 1962?

9 Who was on a TV gig with the editor of *The Times* in 1967?

10 What bespectacled fellow once played with The Red Socks skiffle group but dreamed of another accompaniment?

PRIDE AND FURY

Larry Parnes, the impresario, manager and promoter, discovered a certain Thomas Hicks in the 2 I's coffee bar in Old Compton Street, London, and started a fashion for renaming pop stars with descriptive surnames.

1 Thomas Hicks became Tommy ———?

2 Reginald Smith became Marty ———?

3 Ronald Wycherley became Billy ———?

4 Could Johnny ——— manage to overcome Duffy ———?

5 Terence Neilhams became Adam ———?

6 After Dickie Valentine came Dickie ———?

7 Clive Powell became Georgie ———?

8 Was Vince ——— to get his hands on the Lance ———?

9 Which Rory was accompanied by the Hurricanes?

10 Meanwhile, in the US, who were Billy Medley and Bobby Hartfield?

PSEUDONYMS CORNER

1 Who was born Maurice Cole – on 25 December 1944?

2 Who was born David Cornwell – and took his pen-name from a shoe shop, so he said?

3 Which actress 'bird' took the name of her drama teacher because her own name – Pauline Devaney – had already been used by one half of a scriptwriting team?

4 Who was born Lesley Hornby – and was known as 'Sticks' at school?

5 And what did Nigel Davies turn into?

6 Who was born John Ravenscroft – and hunted after another name?

7 His name wasn't the only thing Daniel Carroll changed. What name did he take?

8 T. Persons changed his name to an equally unusual one. What?

9 Robert Zimmerman honoured a Welsh poet. How?

10 Malcolm Little couldn't write his name, so he called himself . . . ?

SCREEN NAMES

Who was *less* well known as . . .

1 Alexandra Zuck? (Clue: there was a song about her in *Grease*.)

2 Barbara Deeks? (Clue: John Wells once rolled around with her in a Dagenham furniture store.)

3 Maurice Micklewhite? (Clue: he took his new surname from a Gregory Peck film he admired.)

4 Michael Dumble-Smith? (Clue: he started as 'Byron' and later was frank.)

5 Allen Stewart Konigsberg? (Clue: he made his first appearance in *What's New Pussycat?*)

6 Anne Italiano? (Clue: she was an undergraduate.)

7 Thomas Conner?

8 Michael Shalhouz? (Clue: he's making eyes at me.)

9 Samile Diane Friesen? (Clue: Bob and Carol and Ted and . . .)

10 Shirley Beaty?

SLOGANS

1 The pre-credit sequence of the first-ever edition of *Dad's Army* (31 July 1968) was devoted to a slogan of that year. What was it?

2 Why did Harold Wilson reject 'Labour's On the Go' as the party's slogan for the 1964 General Election?

3 What happened in the summer of 1963 to make people say 'Marples Must Go'?

4 What film (released in 1973) was promoted with the slogan 'Where were you in '62?'

5 Who urged, 'Turn on, tune in, drop out'?

6 Who didn't say, 'Don't trust anyone over thirty' and ended up on Wall Street when he was?

7 Who was billed as 'The Golden Girl' of British pop?

8 Who first said that 'Black is Beautiful'?

9 Why did some Berliners find it alarming when John F. Kennedy declared 'Ich bin ein Berliner' ('I am a Berliner')?

10 Which TV programme was promoted with the slogan 'The Weekend Starts Here'?

SPORT

1 Who or what was World Cup Willie?

2 A Southsea greengrocer circumnavigated the globe single-handed and had a rose named after him. Who was he?

3 Who was known as the Golden Boy of British Football?

4 Who won the World Motor Racing Championship and lived to see his wife become godmother to Princess Anne's daughter?

5 Who brought out an LP to help knock out his opponent?

6 What did the England manager and the Archbishop of Canterbury have in common in 1966?

7 What did the Queen do in 1967 that her namesake had done on the same spot in Greenwich 387 years earlier?

8 Where were the Olympic Games held in 1964?

9 Who held the British heavyweight title from 1959 to 1969?

10 How many runs did Garfield Sobers score off one six-ball over in May 1968?

35

STATESIDE

American politicians and their doings . . .

1 What record did President and Mrs Kennedy like to play before going to bed?

2 Which American President showed pressmen scars from his recent gall bladder operation?

3 Who suffered from 'Five O'Clock Shadow'?

4 'AuH$_2$O = H$_2$S' is a formula referring to which American politician?

5 Where was Edward Kennedy the day before the first moon landing?

6 Who was made to sing the 'Alliance for Progress Bossa Nova'?

7 What happened at the Cow Palace, San Francisco, in 1964?

8 Where did Martin Luther King Jr say, 'I have a dream this afternoon', on 23 June 1963?

9 Who said: 'Gentlemen, get the thing straight once and for all: the policeman isn't there to create disorder, the policeman is there to preserve disorder'?

10 Why was Vaughn Meader out of a job after 22 November 1963?

SWINGING LONDON

1 Which supreme arbiter of fashion coined the phrase 'Swinging London'?

2 In which year did *Time* get round to describing the phenomenon?

3 Who used to put his thumb up at the very mention of the word 'swinging'?

4 Before this, who had recorded LPs with the titles 'Songs for Swinging Lovers', 'Songs for Swinging Sellers' and 'Swinging Dors'?

5 Which American recorded the song 'England Swings'?

6 How did Carnaby Street get its name?

7 What was the name of the other fashionable thoroughfare?

8 Name the two waiters who got together to feed the Beautiful People.

9 Which Italian fed the famous at a club named after himself, then at another – and is still at it?

10 Who celebrated the passing of the era with a book entitled *Goodbye, Baby and Amen*?

THEATRE

1 Why was *Oh, Calcutta!* called that?

2 Michael Caine was famous for playing 'Alfie' on the screen but who played him in the original London production of Bill Naughton's play in 1963?

3 What happened at the end of the musical *Hair*?

4 What happened to the Shaftesbury Theatre where *Hair* was first performed in London?

5 After 1968 why was it no longer necessary to omit 'the perversions of the rubber' and to substitute 'the kreurpels and blinges of the rubber'? Or to omit the chamber pot under the bed or for the mock priest to refrain from wearing a crucifix under his snorkel?

6 Where was a nude woman towed across a musicians' gallery giving rise to 'a happening'?

7 Where was *Beyond the Fringe* first performed?

8 In which of the three services did Arnold Wesker set his play *Chips With Everything*?

9 What was the Roundhouse before it became a theatre?

10 What famous show was described by the historian A. J. P. Taylor as 'that profound entertainment'?

TIP OF YOUR TONGUE

1 How do you spell 'Keynsham' – and who used to?

2 Who sang 'Whoop bah oh yeah yeah' before the Beatles got hold of the 'yeah yeah'?

3 What name did Terry Nation invent from looking at the spine of an encyclopedia volume, even if he later denied that this is what he had done?

4 What did *The Times* refer to in its editorial headed 'Blessing in Shades of Green' on 15 July 1967?

5 Where was Motown and why was it so called?

6 What was 'Rachmanism'?

7 What were 'Les Evénements'?

8 'Sexual intercourse began in ———?' (Philip Larkin). Which year?

9 Which Italian phrase described a kind of living?

10 In which film did the word 'grotty' first make an appearance?

WILSONISMS

The sayings of Harold Wilson, British Prime Minister 1964–70 . . .

1 'What we are going to need is one hundred days of ———— action.'

2 What did he reply when asked (on winning the '64 election): 'Do you feel like a Prime Minister?'

3 'A ———— is a long time in politics.'

4 Which constituency did the MP Wilson described as 'a parliamentary leper' come from?

5 What did he say would be over in 'weeks rather than months'?

6 What was the 'tightly knit group of politically motivated men' doing in 1966?

7 What was the occasion of his 'pound in your pocket' remark?

8 'The white heat of the ———— revolution.'

9 'I think that probably the attacks on me in the press and in politics have been worse than any other Prime Minister has had to face, even ———— ————.'

10 According to Mrs Wilson in 1962: 'If Harold has a fault it is that he will drown everything in ———— ————.'

WONDERFULLY TRIVIAL!

1 *Something's Got To Give* 'gave' in 1962. Why?

2 Who was the French Elvis?

3 In the *New Record Mirror* 'Make A Star' Contest of 1962, what did you have to do to win the Bert Weedon Trophy?

4 In the same contest, what did you have to do to win the Brian Matthew Cup?

5 Which was the first 'non-fiction novel'?

6 What was the title of Jenny Fabian's 1969 sociological tract?

7 What was Cherry Vanilla?

8 Who coined the phrase, 'It's been a hard day's night'?

9 What were 'TAM' ratings?

10 Who dropped an 's' in the Sixties and restored it in the Seventies?

ANSWERS

ABSOLUTELY TRIVIAL!

1 Diabetes.

2 Portugal.

3 The first wife of Jimmy Hanley (of ITV's *Jim's Inn*) was Dinah Sheridan (who appeared in the '50s film *Genevieve*). Their wonderful daughter, Jenny Hanley, was a presenter of ITV's *Magpie* from 1968.

4 Billy J. Kramer. He was one of four finalists miming to 'I'll Keep You Satisfied' but did not find favour with the judge, Chris Sandford, then of *Coronation Street*.

5 The Aardvarks. If they had ever had a hit they would have been listed before Abba and ABC in the *Guinness Book of British Hit Singles* which Tim co-edits.

6 He did the male voices for the children's TV series *The Flowerpot Men*. A group called The Flowerpot Men had a hit with 'Let's Go To San Francisco', though they probably had a different sort of pot in mind.

7 A Vernon's Girl.

8 He is not a Cockney. He was born in Lincolnshire.

9 His wife Angela was a 'Beat the Clock' hostess (with Bruce Forsyth) on *Sunday Night at the London Palladium*.

10 John Lennon, Paul McCartney, George Harrison and Stuart Sutcliffe – the original line-up of The Silver Beatles.

ADS

1 Terence Brook. He appeared as a Sinatra-clone in the classic 1960 campaign for Strand cigarettes. The 'Lonely Man Theme' was a hit record, but the fags flopped.

2 TWA.

3 '. . . Shirt You Don't Iron.'

4 National Benzole.

5 Because of the Esso Campaign 'Put a Tiger in Your Tank'.

6 In a 1962 'Peanuts' book by Charles M. Schultz – *Happiness Is A Warm Puppy*.

7 'Cadbury's Dairy Milk' (chocolate).

8 Consulate cigarettes ('Menthol-fresh . . . cool, clear Consulate').

9 Norman Vaughan in TV ads for Cadbury's Roses chocolates.

10 Katie, the Oxo lady. (She later changed her name to Katie Holland.)

BEATLEMANIA

1 Mike McGear, Paul McCartney's brother, was part of The Scaffold who had a No. 1 hit in 1968 with 'Lily the Pink'.

2 Fred Lennon, John's errant father who surfaced in 1965, made the record, and then disappeared again.

3 Brian Epstein, the Beatles' manager, was given this title – much to his annoyance – by the American disc-jockey in 1964.

4 John Lennon and Yoko Ono, March 1969.

5 Beethoven.

6 Schubert.

7 Winston.

8 'That's near us.'

9 People who don't like music (in the film *Yellow Submarine*).

10 Not one major crime was committed.

BEEB

1 *Mogul* – the name of the oil company.

2 (a) Robert Hardy (b) Sean Connery.

3 *All in the Family*.

4 Barry Bucknell.

5 'United Network Command for Law and Enforcement' – and not, 'United Nations Campaign Against Lesbian Elephants', as suggested by Willie Rushton.

6 Cartoon mascots promoting BBC2 when the new channel opened in 1964. The first night was ruined by a power cut in London.

7 One is called 'old Ned' and the other is old Ned Sherrin. Both programmes were first broadcast in 1962.

8 Hercules.

9 Hugh Carleton-Greene became simply Hugh Greene when knighted. He was the inspiring Director-General of the BBC in its most adventurous years, 1960–9.

10 The first was a 1959 pop show (successor to *Six-Five Special*), the second an anthology of prose and poetry broadcast in 1963.

BESTSELLERS

1 30.

2 Three shillings and sixpence.

3 Mason Hoffenburg and Terry Southern. *Candy* was first published under this pseudonym by the Olympia Press, Paris, in 1958. It was published in the US under their real names in *c*.1965.

4 *Thunderball.*

5 Kingsley Amis.

6 John Calder.

7 Rt Revd John Robinson, Bishop of Woolwich.

8 'Portnoy's Complaint' – from the novel of that name by Philip Roth.

9 *A Spaniard in the Works* (1965).

10 *Valley of the Dolls* by Jacqueline Susann.

BOND WOMEN

1 Ursula Andress.

2 Daniela Bianchi.

3 'Rosa Klebb'.

4 Honor Blackman.

5 She met her screen end embalmed in gold.

6 Claudine Auger.

7 Mie Hama

8 Jacqueline Bisset.

9 Diana Rigg. The character was killed in a motor accident shortly after marrying James Bond.

10 Lois Maxwell played M's secretary who never got her man.

CATCHPHRASES

1 'Sock it to me.' And eventually they did.

2 Janice Nicholls, the Black Country girl who found fame rating discs on *Thank Your Lucky Stars*. 'The Wednesbury Madison' was the flip side of her own record, 'I'll Give it Five'.

3 *Goldfinger*.

4 David Frost in *That Was The Week That Was*.

5 Bruce Forsyth in *Sunday Night at the London Palladium*.

6 A German helmet.

7 *Round the Horne*.

8 *The Perry Como Show*.

9 The younger to the older in *Steptoe and Son*.

10 Bob Monkhouse in *The Golden Shot*.

FAB GEAR

1 Mary Quant, the fashion designer and entrepreneur who started Bazaar, what may have been the first 'boutique', in Chelsea, as early as 1955.

2 1967.

3 Hung them on their hips to make 'hipsters'. He was a leading light behind Carnaby Street and the fashions of the 1960s.

4 When you go into a menswear shop to buy a tie and they take your inside leg measurement.

5 Vidal Sassoon.

6 Wore them on their feet (pointed shoes).

7 Jean Shrimpton ('the Face of the 60s'). Her Penzance hotel was so described in the 1985 *Good Hotel Guide*.

8 Michael Fish, menswear designer, created the fashion for kipper (wide) ties.

9 Barbara Hulanicki.

10 A trouser suit.

FADS

1 1962; £639 inc. tax.

2 1965.

3 Longleat, the seat of Marquis of Bath in Wiltshire – really the first such lion park of any size outside Kenya. It set the trend for safari parks.

4 Gonks – a soft toy, usually egg-shaped, with arms and legs attached.

5 *International Times* – an 'underground' newspaper.

6 The celebrated 1969 squat by several hundred people in an empty 100 room mansion.

7 Yippies (politically active hippies).

8 Short for 'Modernists'.

9 A district in San Francisco – the centre of 'flower-power', and very psychedelic . . .

10 L.S.D.

FILMS

1 Dick Lester, who subsequently directed *The Knack, A Hard Day's Night, Help!* etc.

2 George Lazenby, whose screen appearances up to then had chiefly consisted of advertising chocolate on TV, played James Bond in *On Her Majesty's Secret Service* in 1969.

3 Julie Christie.

4 Jean Shrimpton.

5 Thomas Crapper Ltd, sanitary engineers by appointment to King George V.

6 Maryon Wilson Park, Woolwich.

7 Joyce Redman.

8 Rugby league football.

9 *The Wrong Box.*

10 A nose job.

FROSTIE

1 'Paradine'.

2 The Revd W. J. Paradine Frost was a Methodist minister.

3 Mona.

4 *Let's Twist on the Riviera*.

5 David Kernan, Lance Percival, Millicent Martin, William Rushton, Kenneth Cope, Bernard Levin.

6 Peter Cook.

7 George Martin (of Beatles fame).

8 None of them. His first wife, much later, was Lynne Frederick, widow of Peter Sellers.

9 Jonathan Miller.

10 They had breakfast with him at the Connaught Hotel. Paul McCartney had also been invited but pleaded a previous engagement.

GROUPS

1 Because they are the *Brothers Gibb*.

2 Vibes. According to the Bonzo Dog Doo-dah Band.

3 Trigger – silly!

4 Acker Bilk with 'Stranger on the Shore' (also the title of the TV series). The diminutive actress was Denise Coffey.

5 Dozy, Beaky, Mick and Tich.

6 Tottenham. They came from there.

7 Mickey Dolenz, Davy Jones, Mike Naismith and Peter Tork.

8 Davy Jones.

9 Mickey Dolenz, using the name Mickey Braddock.

10 It is said to be Latin for 'beyond these things' (sometimes also spelt 'Procol').

GRUESOME TWOSOMES

1 British actress Judy Carne (born Joyce Botteril) – the 'Sock it to me' girl of *Rowan Martin's Laugh-In* was married to Burt Reynolds.

2 Thomas Balogh and Nicholas Kaldor – economic advisers to the Labour government from 1964. Both were created Life Peers.

3 The Duke and Duchess of Argyll.

4 Jack Cotton and Charles Clore were both property tycoons.

5 Peter Asher of pop duo 'Peter and Gordon' was the brother of actress Jane Asher, Paul McCartney's girlfriend.

6 Catherine Deneuve (they married in 1965).

7 The French actress Anouk Aimée. She married Albert Finney.

8 Reggie and Ronnie Kray, criminals. The snake was named after Leonard 'Nipper' Read, the policeman who eventually brought them to justice.

9 The Jay Twins – Helen and Catherine. Their father was Douglas Jay, President of the Board of Trade, and their brother was Peter, a future British Ambassador to Washington.

10 Richard Burton and Elizabeth Taylor in the film of Edward Albee's *Who's Afraid of Virginia Woolf?*

HACKS

1 Jim Anderson, Felix Dennis and Richard Neville.

2 1966.

3 The Profumo Affair, in 1963.

4 1964.

5 Christopher Booker.

6 *Nova*.

7 Compact.

8 Cecil King (because he was not the proprietor of the *Daily Mirror*, only chairman of the newspaper group).

9 It said he had nothing to do with it.

10 The New Journalism.

I LIKE THE BACKING

1 Dakotas.

2 Band.

3 Crickets.

4 Luvvers.

5 Bruvvers.

6 Outlaws.

7 Union Gap.

8 First Edition.

9 Stingers.

10 Kinks – or, just possibly, if you were thinking of another group – the Button-Down Brass.

LENNON AND McCARTNEY

1 'She Loves You', No. 1 in August 1963.

2 Laurence Olivier as Richard III.

3 As a vicar.

4 Not only their most recorded song but probably also the most recorded song by any composer. There are more than 1,000 versions.

5 'A Day in the Life'.

6 'Abbey Road'.

7 'Let It Be'.

8 Julian Lennon, John's son (Julian → Jules → Jude).

9 'Taxman' – Mister Wilson and Mister Heath.

10 Four thousand (in 'A Day in the Life').

LIVERPOOL

1 Allen Ginsberg.

2 Huyton (Harold Wilson's constituency).

3 Gerry and the Pacemakers.

4 The Roman Catholic Cathedral of Christ the King.

5 A Salvation Army Children's Home.

6 Knotty Ash (according to Ken Dodd).

7 In the traditional song she was a tart who stole her customers' trousers. Alas, Lionel Bart's musical *Maggie May* (1964) made little mark.

8 ⅔ false. Those named were 'the Liverpool Poets'. Roger McGough was also a member of The Scaffold.

9 Nerys Hughes and Polly James.

10 Flap their wings. (They don't do it often.)

M.O.R.

1 Matt Monro.

2 Ernie (as sung by Benny Hill).

3 Depends what you mean by singing, of course – but Alan Freeman did not even attempt singing on 'The Madison'.

4 Anyone singing 'My Way' – usually Frank Sinatra or Dorothy Squires.

5 Burt Bacharach.

6 A group of London dockers who had come to lend support to Enoch Powell's anti-immigration views.

7 *Breakfast at Tiffany's.*

8 Wink Martindale.

9 Wobble board.

10 Mary Hopkin.

MOVIES

1 It's *west* of Java.

2 *One Million Years BC* – there was no dialogue.

3 Mike Sarne – who sang 'Come Outside' – acted opposite Bardot in *Two Weeks in September* and directed West in *Myra Breckinridge*. After which . . . ?

4 Julie Andrews appeared as child-star on the 1950s radio show *Educating Archie* (Archie Andrews was a ventriloquist's dummy) and listed her 'Favourite Things' in *The Sound of Music* which some people saw scores of times.

5 *Barefoot in the Park*.

6 *Cleopatra*.

7 *The Misfits*.

8 Jacqueline Bissett.

9 Warren Beatty.

10 *The Thomas Crown Affair*.

NEWS TOENAILS

1 Approximately £2½ million.

2 Goldie, a golden eagle, who escaped from his cage at London Zoo, was free for twelve days.

3 The cutting of railway services following Dr Richard Beeching's report in 1963.

4 Hurricane 'Hattie' caused widespread destruction.

5 She sang 'Happy Birthday' to him.

6 Telstar was the name given to two low-altitude communications satellites launched by the US in 1962–3. Joe Meek produced the instrumental 'Telstar' by the Tornadoes which was a No. 1 hit in the UK and the US.

7 The world's first passenger Hovercraft service.

8 Michael Collins. He stayed in the command module while Neil Armstrong and Buzz Aldrin stepped on to the surface of the moon, the first men to do so.

9 Goya's portrait of the first Duke was stolen from the National Gallery in 1961. It had still not been found at the time when it was shown among Dr No's possessions in the 1962 film. It was recovered in 1965.

10 Prince Charles when a 14-year-old pupil at Gordonstoun.

NICKNAMES

1 Joan Bakewell was so dubbed by Frank Muir. She appeared on *Late-Night Line-Up*, one of BBC2 TV's first colour programmes.

2 Brenda Lee.

3 Alan Freeman, the radio DJ, who began presenting *Pick of the Pops* in 1962. He was given the nickname not because he always fluffed his lines but because of an old pullover he wore which went all fluffy after it was dry-cleaned.

4 Daniel Cohn-Bendit, a leading figure in the 1968 student uprising in France. A West German, he was studying at Nanterre University. More usually known as 'Red Dany'. Danny La Rue, the Irish-born drag artist, was well known by this time.

5 Graham Kerr, British-born TV cookery expert, popular with the ladies. He made programmes in Canada which were then shown all over the world. He made at least £3 million and then, in 1972, he suddenly retired in search of truth.

6 David Hamilton, the DJ – so named by Ken Dodd.

7 Jean Shrimpton, model.

8 Harold Wilson.

9 Lt-Col Colin Mitchell – mentioned in dispatches during the Aden emergency in 1967.

10 After the trick vocal effects he used on his first disc 'Ain't Got No Home' in 1956.

OLDIES BUT GOLDIES

1 MacArthur Park, in the song by Jim Webb. It is an actual park in the centre of Los Angeles.

2 'Fings Ain't What They Used T'Be'.

3 Frankie Howerd and June Whitfield.

4 'I can't get no satisfaction.'

5 *The Millionairess*.

6 Frank and Nancy Sinatra recorded 'Something Stupid' together and had a No. 1 hit in April 1967.

7 'You'll Never Walk Alone' from *Carousel* became a football anthem in Liverpool.

8 George Harrison's 'My Sweet Lord' – there was a court case about it and he lost.

9 In 'A Whiter Shade of Pale'.

10 Eddie Cochran.

OTHER CHANNEL

1 *Police Surgeon* (1960) was developed into *The Avengers* (1961/2).

2 Because (played by Diana Rigg) she added 'M appeal' (= Man appeal) to *The Avengers*.

3 *Nice Time* – a folksy bit of froth and eccentricity from Granada (1968).

4 Tony Warren.

5 'Who will buy my red oranges?' – arranged by Johnny Hawksworth.

6 Cathy McGowan, Keith Fordyce.

7 Alastair Burnet and Andrew Gardner.

8 Portmeirion.

9 Al Martine.

10 Bernard Braden. ITV's *On the Braden Beat* became the BBC's *Braden Week*. Braden eventually had to pull out when the BBC felt that the presenter of a consumer-oriented show was not the best person to advertise Campbell's Soup. Thus was the way cleared for Braden's researcher, Esther Rantzen, to front her own version, *That's Life*.

PERMISSIVE SOCIETY

1 Marianne Faithfull, the singer, was Mick Jagger's girlfriend from 1967–70. She is also widely believed to have enjoyed Mars bars.

2 Homosexuality between consenting adults (in England and Wales only) following the passing of the Sexual Offences Act.

3 His bottom appeared in her 1967 film made up entirely of people's naked nates. She believed your backside accurately reflected your personality.

4 Honor Blackman and Patrick MacNee (in their roles 'Cathy Gale' and 'John Steed' from *The Avengers* TV series) recorded a song in 1964 called 'Kinky Boots'. The lyrics were by Herbert Kretzmer, and serves him right.

5 The Maharishi Mahesh Yogi. John Lennon considered him to be a randy old goat but was dissuaded from naming him in the song.

6 Lord Astor. In June 1963, at a magistrates court hearing, it was stated that he had denied her allegations that they had slept together.

7 Kenneth Tynan during a discussion on theatre censorship in BBC TV's *Not So Much A Programme, More A Way Of Life*, November 1965.

8 In Antonioni's *Blow-Up*, David Hemming romps with a couple of naked girls in a photographer's studio. He keeps his trousers on, however.

9 *Je T'Aime . . . Moi Non Plus* by Jane Birkin and Serge Gainsbourg.

10 *Lady Chatterley's Lover* by D. H. Lawrence. Penguin Books were prosecuted for publishing an obscene book in 1961 but were acquitted. The Bishop of Woolwich, John Robinson, made this remark when called as a defence witness.

PERSONALITIES

1 Patrick Campbell – surely the first ever TV personality to have a (genuine) stammer?

2 He was an American agent in London who became a resident chatterer on the same programme.

3 He was Commander of South Vietnam's police force. He shot dead an unarmed Vietcong suspect in front of photographers during the Tet offensive of 1968.

4 She won £152,000 on Littlewoods football pools and said, 'I'm going to spend, spend, spend.' And she did – until it was all gone.

5 Paul Getty.

6 Earl Mountbatten's.

7 Wearing silly hats at Ascot.

8 Sheila Scott.

9 Bo Diddley was an American singer/instrumentalist; 'Bo Dudley' was the name adopted by Dudley Moore for a record he made in 1966 with Peter Cook.

10 Anthony Armstrong-Jones and Princess Margaret.

POLITICS

1 Independent (though he retired on the eve of poll in favour of the Liberal candidate); 45 votes.

2 Harold Macmillan spoke the words in a speech. *Private Eye* added a backing and put the result out on disc.

3 Viscount Hailsham who became Quintin Hogg (later Lord Hailsham).

4 The Earl of Home who became Sir Alec Douglas-Home (and later Lord Home). Lord Dunglass.

5 John Bird on TV satire shows.

6 When Harold Macmillan was speaking before the United Nations General Assembly in 1960. Nikita Khruschev interrupted him, at one point, by taking off his shoe and banging it on his desk. Macmillan drily asked for a translation of his 'remarks'.

7 Harold Wilson's distinctive mackintoshes were supplied by Joseph Kagan. This person was created Lord Kagan in Wilson's resignation honours list in 1976 and gaoled for fraud.

8 'E. L. Wisty', the droll character played by Peter Cook, originally in *Beyond the Fringe* and later on TV.

9 Viscount Stansgate.

10 For the removal of a prostate obstruction.

POP NAMES

1 Dusty Springfield (whose brother became composer Tom Springfield).

2 Alvin Stardust. Bernard Jewry was a member of the Fentones who backed the first Shane Fenton, and when he died, took over the name. In the early 70s he took the name Stardust. His wife Lisa Goddard calls him Bert and his mother remains confused.

3 Cilla Black. A Liverpool newspaper got her name wrong and the rest, as they say, is history . . .

4 Ringo Starr. He got his name from his mum because of his habit of wearing rings. He rather liked the surname 'Starr' because it would enable him to top the bill at New Brighton in anything called 'Starr-time'.

5 Jess Conrad. 'This Pullover' was once voted one of the worst pop songs ever recorded.

6 Chubby Checker (Chubby = Fats; Checker = Domino).

7 Engelbert Humperdinck was born Arnold Dorsey and first started appearing as Gerry Dorsey.

8 Tom Jones. He was born Thomas Jones Woodward, then became 'Tommy Scott, the Twisting Vocalist', and finally settled on a name akin to the title-role in a noted 1963 film (he wore the pigtail for a time, too).

9 Lulu. Her younger sister, Edwina Laurie, stuck to the family name when she entered show business in the early '80s.

10 Tiny Tim. What's more the falsetto singer surprised everyone by fathering a child.

POP RADIO

1 Tommy Vance, so billed in the early days of Radio 1. He took the name 'Tommy Vance' when working in the US because a radio station had some spare jingles incorporating the name.

2 Tony Blackburn; 'Flowers in the Rain' by The Move; he recorded this song with some success and it was included on an album called 'Tony Blackburn Sings', just in case there was any doubt what he was doing.

3 DJ David Hamilton (Pilditch was his original name) first found fame as a TV announcer who signed off with this line. A song was written to incorporate it.

4 Emperor Rosko. Joe Pasternak was a film producer.

5 Radio announcer Pat Doody's baby son Ian recorded the jingle which was used by Dave Cash (born Dave Wish).

6 He named his pirate ship 'Radio Caroline' after her. It first broadcast from the high seas on 28 March 1963.

7 Simon Dee (for it is he) and Tony Brandon (ditto) both, separately, recorded versions of the song 'Julie'.

8 A chipmunk-voiced character who introduced Jimmy Young's recipe spot on Radio 1 with cries of 'What's the recipe today, Jim?' and 'This is what you do!' BBC studio manager Max Alcock was one of the two voices speeded up to get the desired effect.

9 Keith Fordyce. (Or Keith Fordyce Marriott – which is his real name.)

10 Brian Matthew – introducing the Light Programme's *Saturday Club*.

POP SINGERS

1 Sandie Shaw, who sang barefoot.

2 David Sutch, known as 'Screaming Lord Sutch'. The first of his many appearances at by-elections was in 1963 at Stratford-upon-Avon. He stood as the National Teenage Candidate in the by-election caused by the resignation of John Profumo.

3 Nina Van Pallandt, half of the Nina and Frederick duo, was later a companion of Clifford Irving who made out that he had acquired the autobiography of Howard Hughes.

4 David Bowie.

5 Wendy Richard, who later played Miss Brahms in *Are You Being Served?*

6 Because he had changed his name to P. J. Proby.

7 John Leyton, who later returned to acting in such films as *The Great Escape, Von Ryan's Express* and *Krakatoa, East of Java.*

8 Adam Faith discussed religion with him.

9 Mick Jagger was flown by helicopter to join William Rees-Mogg for a discussion on drugs for ITV's *World in Action.*

10 Freddie Garrity, of Freddie and the Dreamers.

PRIDE AND FURY

1 Steele.

2 Wilde.

3 Fury.

4 Gentle; Power.

5 Faith.

6 Pride.

7 Fame.

8 Eager; Fortune.

9 Storm.

10 The Righteous Brothers.

PSEUDONYMS
CORNER

1 Kenny Everett, the disc-jockey.

2 Writer John Le Carré (the shoe shop story was a fabrication, he later admitted).

3 Polly James of *Liver Birds* fame took her new surname from James Grout, the actor. The other Pauline Devaney wrote another sit-com, *All Gas and Gaiters*, with Edwin Apps.

4 Twiggy.

5 Justin de Villeneuve, boyfriend, agent and discoverer (1964) of Twiggy.

6 John Peel, the disc-jockey.

7 Danny La Rue, the female impersonator.

8 Truman Capote.

9 By calling himself Bob Dylan.

10 Malcolm X.

SCREEN NAMES

1 Sandra Dee. The song in *Grease* is called 'Look at me, I'm Sandra Dee'.

2 Barbara Windsor.

3 Michael Caine (rather than 'Michael Mutiny') after *The Caine Mutiny*.

4 Michael Crawford played a character called 'Byron' in the satire show *BBC3* and in the '70s played 'Frank Spencer' in *Some Mothers Do Have 'Em*.

5 Woody Allen.

6 Anne Bancroft (who starred in *The Graduate*).

7 Sean Connery.

8 Omar Sharif.

9 Dyan Cannon.

10 Shirley Maclaine (Warren Beatty's sister – he added a 't').

SLOGANS

1 'I'm Backing Britain' – slogan of a short-lived campaign to make people work harder. Arthur Lowe as Captain Mainwaring was shown as chairman of an I'm Backing Britain committee before the series got down to reliving the Home Guard days of the Second World War.

2 He thought it would indicate the party was prone to diarrhoea. 'Let's go with Labour' was chosen instead.

3 Ernest Marples, Minister of Transport, imposed a 50 mph speed limit on roads at peak holiday weekends (the culmination of a number of measures restricting motorists).

4 *American Graffiti.*

5 Dr Timothy Leary, guru of drug culture, 1967.

6 Jerry Rubin. Although often attributed to him, it was first uttered by Jack Weinberg in 1964.

7 Kathy Kirby.

8 Stokely Carmichael in 1966.

9 A 'Berliner' is also the name of a doughnut.

10 *Ready Steady Go!*

SPORT

1 The England mascot in the 1966 World Cup.

2 Sir Alec Rose.

3 Georgie Best, who played for Manchester United in the '60s.

4 Jackie Stewart.

5 Cassius Clay (as he then was) whose LP 'I Am the Greatest' appeared in the run up to his World Heavyweight Championship fight with Sonny Liston whom he beat in February 1964.

6 They were both called 'Ramsey' – Michael and Sir Alf.

7 Knighted a mariner – in her case, round-the-world yachtsman Francis Chichester. Elizabeth I knighted Francis Drake.

8 Melbourne.

9 Henry Cooper.

10 36 (the most runs ever scored off one over).

STATESIDE

1 *Camelot* – the musical which opened in the month before he became President and which provided the name for the romantic view of his presidency.

2 Lyndon B. Johnson.

3 Richard M. Nixon – particularly in the TV debates with John F. Kennedy in 1960.

4 Barry M. Goldwater. In 1964 he was the unsuccessful Republican challenger to President Johnson. The formula means: 'Gold + water = hydrogen sulphide'.

5 Chappaquiddick.

6 President Kennedy. The 1962 EP 'Sing Along With JFK' comprised clips from his 1961 Inaugural address with musical backing.

7 Barry Goldwater accepted the Republican Party's nomination.

8 Detroit. (His more famous Washington version of the speech was given on 28 August 1963.)

9 Mayor Daley of Chicago during the disturbances surrounding the 1968 Democratic Convention.

10 He impersonated President Kennedy (who was killed on that day) – most notably on the highly successful 1962 album 'The First Family'.

SWINGING LONDON

1 Diana Vreeland, *Weekend Telegraph*, 30 April 1965.

2 1965.

3 Norman Vaughan, host of ITV's *Sunday Night at the London Palladium* from 1962. And he put his thumb down at the mention of the word 'dodgy'.

4 Frank Sinatra; Peter Sellers; Diana Dors.

5 Roger Miller.

6 Richard Tyler, a seventeenth-century property developer, had a house called Karnaby House thereabouts.

7 King's Road, Chelsea.

8 Mario and Franco.

9 Alvaro Maccioni at Alvaro's, then the Club dell'Arethusa and now at La Famiglia and La Nassa.

10 David Bailey and Peter Evans.

THEATRE

1 Kenneth Tynan's 1969 revue took its title from the French saying 'Oh, quel cul t'as' which broadly speaking means 'What a lovely bum you've got' and sounds a bit like 'Calcutta' when spoken quickly.

2 John Neville.

3 No, they didn't take their clothes off. Members of the audience danced with the cast on stage. On one occasion Princess Anne was among those who joined in.

4 The roof fell in.

5 The Lord Chamberlain's powers of censorship over the English stage were abolished. Hence, his alterations to the script of Spike Milligan's 1963 comedy *The Bed-Sitting Room* were no longer imposed.

6 At the Edinburgh Festival Drama Conference in 1963. A happening was the name given to an improvised theatrical experience, usually rather disorganised and embarrassing to watch.

7 As part of the 1960 Edinburgh Festival. It was not part of the 'Fringe' – hence it was 'Beyond the Fringe' and part of the official festival.

8 The RAF.

9 A railway engine shed.

10 Theatre Workshop's *Oh What a Lovely War*.

TIP OF YOUR TONGUE

1 Horace Bachelor, inventor of the 'Infra-Draw' method of doing the football pools, always used to have his address spelled out – 'Dept X, Keynsham, that's K–E–Y–N–S–H–A–M, Bristol' – in Radio Luxembourg commercials.

2 Helen Shapiro in 'Walking Back to Happiness'.

3 'Dalek', in the TV series *Dr Who*, from 1963. The encyclopedia spine was supposed to have had on it 'DAL – LEK' but he later confessed he had only made this story up for a journalist and, really, the name just occurred to him accidentally.

4 Ecstasy and drugs.

5 Detroit, nicknamed 'Motortown'.

6 Exploitation of tenants by a landlord of slum property – named after Perec Rachman, Polish-born London property-owner who died in 1962.

7 'The events' – a euphemism for the student uprising in France during the spring of 1968.

8 1963.

9 'La Dolce Vita' – 'the sweet life' (film title, 1960).

10 *A Hard Day's Night* (the word is sometimes said to have been coined by Alun Owen, the scriptwriter).

WILSONISMS

1 Dynamic.

2 'No, I feel like a drink.'

3 Week.

4 Smethwick (referring to a Tory who was thought to have fought a racist campaign).

5 The Rhodesian rebellion.

6 Running a national dock strike.

7 The devaluation of the pound in 1967.

8 Technological.

9 Lloyd George.

10 HP Sauce.

WONDERFULLY TRIVIAL!

1 Marilyn Monroe's health led to her pulling out of the picture. Doris Day was announced to replace her, but the film was never made.

2 Johnny Halliday.

3 Play the guitar.

4 Sing well.

5 *In Cold Blood* by Truman Capote, 1966.

6 *Groupie.*

7 An American groupie.

8 Ringo Starr, although John Lennon may have said it first.

9 A system of 'television audience measurement' once used in the UK.

10 Keith Richard(s) of the Rolling Stones.

Also available in Unwin Paperbacks

Quotable Trivia *Nigel Rees*	£1.75	☐
Showbiz Trivia *Nigel Rees*	£1.75	☐

Other titles of interest

Amazing! *David Farris*	£1.50	☐
Games of Logic *Pierre Berloquin*	£1.95	☐
Geometric Games *Pierre Berloquin*	£1.95	☐
The Incredible Quiz Book *Ian Messiter*	£1.75	☐
Quintessential Quizzes *Norman Hickman*	£1.95	☐
More Quintessential Quizzes *Norman Hickman*	£1.95	☐
Sunday Times Book of Brain Teasers 2		
Victor Bryant & Ronald Postill	£1.95	☐
The Ultimate Crossword Book *Michael Curl*	£2.95	☐

All these books are available at your local bookshop or newsagent, or can be ordered direct by post. Just tick the titles you want and fill in the form below.

Name ....

Address ....

....

....

Write to Unwin Cash Sales, PO Box 11, Falmouth, Cornwall TR10 9EN. Please enclose remittance to the value of the cover price plus:

UK: 55p for the first book plus 22p for the second book, thereafter 14p for each additional book ordered to a maximum charge or £1.75.

BFPO and EIRE: 55p for the first book plus 22p for the second book and 14p for the next 7 books and thereafter 8p per book.

OVERSEAS: £1.00 for the first book plus 25p per copy for each additional book.

Unwin Paperbacks reserve the right to show new retail prices on covers, which may differ from those previously advertised in the text or elsewhere. Postage rates are also subject to revision.